SOUTH PARK

GUIDE TO LIFE

KYLE:

REMEMBER WHEN LIFE USED TO BE SIMPLE AND COOL?

CARTMAN:

NOT REALLY.

SOUTH PARK GUIDE TO LIFE

CREATED BY
TREY PARKER AND MATT STONE

RUNNING PRESS
PHILADELPHIA • LONDON

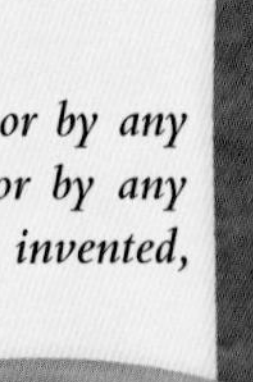

Printed in China

9 8 7 6 5 4 3

Digit on the right indicates the number of this printing

Library of Congress Control Number: 2008926945

ISBN 978-0-7624-3570-8

Design by Joshua McDonnell, Karen Onorato, Richard Kelly, Jonathan Weed
Edited by Greg Jones
Typography: Newsouthpark

Running Press Book Publishers
2300 Chestnut Street
Philadelphia, PA 19103-4371

Visit us on the web!
www.runningpress.com

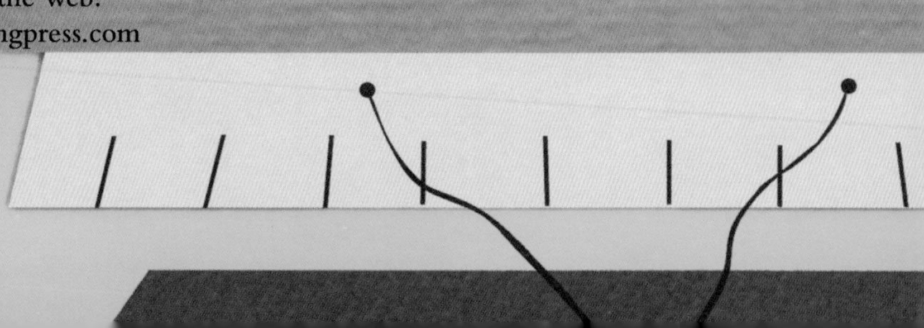

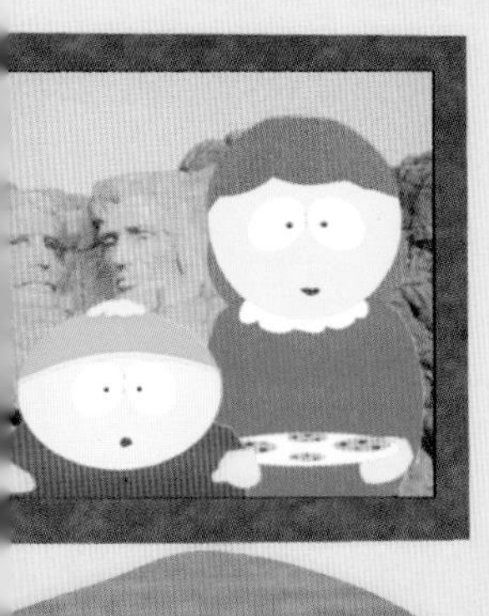

FOREWORD

SOUTH PARK AIRED FOR THE FIRST TIME ON AUGUST 13, 1997. FOR THE PAST 11 AND A HALF YEARS, MILLIONS HAVE ENJOYED THE BITING, SATIRIC HUMOR THAT IS THE SHOW'S SIGNATURE STYLE.

TRUE *SOUTH PARK* FANS KNOW THE GENESIS OF *SOUTH PARK* WAS A SHORT PIECE OF ANIMATION CALLED, "THE SPIRIT OF CHRISTMAS." IT WAS IN THIS GROUNDBREAKING SHORT THAT I, BRIAN BOITANO, BECAME TIED TO *SOUTH PARK* FOREVER. WHEN THE CHIPS WERE DOWN FOR OUR FOUR HEROES—STAN, KYLE, CARTMAN AND KENNY—THEY TURNED TO ME FOR ADVICE ABOUT HOW TO SAVE CHRISTMAS FROM SANTA AND JESUS. WHAT THE BOYS KNEW FROM THE VERY BEGINNING WAS THAT WHEN TIMES ARE TOUGH, YOU SHOULD ALWAYS ASK, "WHAT WOULD BRIAN BOITANO DO?"

ONCE AGAIN THE CREATORS OF *SOUTH PARK* HAVE CALLED ON ME FOR HELP.

MANY PEOPLE THINK OF *SOUTH PARK* AS SIMPLY A FUNNY, CRUDE CARTOON. WELL IT'S UP TO ME TO SET THE RECORD STRAIGHT. *SOUTH PARK* IS MORE THAN JUST A BUNCH OF FART JOKES. IN EACH AND EVERY *SOUTH PARK* EPISODE THERE ARE LIFE LESSONS TO BE FOUND.

FOR EXAMPLE, BECAUSE OF *SOUTH PARK*, MANY OF YOU HAVE LEARNED ABOUT ME AND HOW I APPROACH STICKY SITUATIONS. LIKE THE *SOUTH PARK* KIDS, I WANT TO CONTINUE TO INSPIRE YOU TO DO THE RIGHT THING IN YOUR OWN LIVES. ALWAYS REMEMBER THAT YOU, TOO, CAN BUILD SOME PYRAMIDS; AND WHEN YOU'RE FIGHTING GRIZZLY BEARS, ALWAYS USE YOUR MAGICAL FIRE BREATH. AT TIMES EVEN I HAVE TO ASK MYSELF: 'WHAT WOULD I DO?'

WELL, IN THIS CASE, I WOULD READ THIS BOOK. IF YOU DON'T READ THIS BOOK, AND READ IT QUICKLY, I WILL KICK YOUR ASS. I PROBABLY ALREADY KICKED AN ASS OR TWO IN THE TIME IT TOOK YOU TO READ THIS.

MANY APPLES,

BRIAN BOITANO

I'VE LEARNED SOMETHING TODAY

SCHPECK: USING LOGIC AND REASON ISN'T ENOUGH. YOU HAVE TO BE A DICK TO EVERYONE WHO DOESN'T THINK LIKE YOU.

KYLE: SWEARING CAN BE FUN, BUT DOING IT ALL THE TIME CAUSES A LOT OF PROBLEMS.

SHELLEY: YOU CAN'T RUN FROM YOUR PAST, **TURD!** APOLOGIZE AND MAKE AMENDS.

CHEF: **YOU CAN'T TEACH A GAY DOG STRAIGHT TRICKS.**

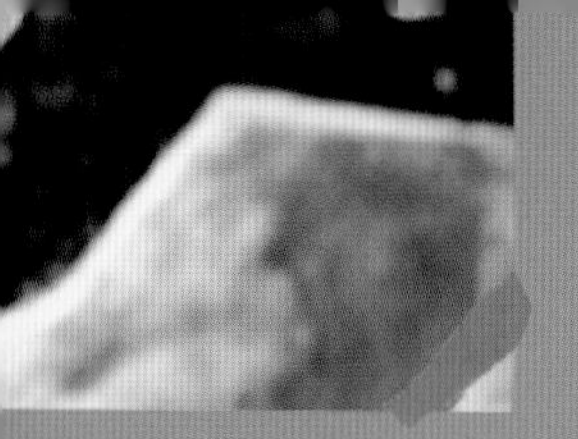

MR. GARRISON:

REMEMBER: THERE ARE NO STUPID QUESTIONS, JUST STUPID PEOPLE.

KYLE: REAL LIFE IS SO BORING AND STUPID!
CHIPS
CHIPS
ZOOP

CARTMAN: POOR PEOPLE TEND TO LIVE IN CLUSTERS.

CARTMAN:

REAL GUITARS ARE FOR OLD PEOPLE.

SUPER ADVENTURE CLUB LEADER:
COOL PEOPLE LEAVE BEFORE THEY'VE OVERSTAYED THEIR WELCOME.

PETA LEADER:

NEARLY EVERY ELECTION SINCE THE BEGINNING OF TIME HAS BEEN BETWEEN SOME DOUCHE AND SOME TURD. THEY'RE THE ONLY PEOPLE WHO SUCK UP ENOUGH TO MAKE IT THAT FAR IN POLITICS.

EARTH DAY PRESIDENT:

NOTHING MATTERS MORE THAN SAVING THE PLANET FROM REPUBLICANS.

CARTMAN:

LIFE GOES BY PRETTY FAST. IF YOU DON'T STOP AND LOOK AROUND ONCE IN A WHILE, AND DO WHATEVER YOU WANT ALL THE TIME, YOU COULD MISS IT.

CARTMAN:
I'M GONNA SPEND MY WHOLE CHILDHOOD EATING WHAT I WANT AND DOIN' DRUGS WHEN I WANT! WHATEVER! I'LL DO WHAT I WANT!

WE'RE GONNA MAKE SO MUCH MONEY YOU GUYS

THE UNITED STATES OF AMERICA

BEBE: THE ONLY THING MORE IMPORTANT THAN BEING RICH IS BEING FAMOUS.

RANDY: THERE'S MORE TO LIFE THAN PROFITS.
CHIEF RUNS WITH PREMISE: WELL, LIKE WHAT?
RANDY: WELL, LIKE, YOU KNOW, SLURPEES™ AND STUFF.

THE WORLD NEWS
T

TOKEN: WHY DO WE HAVE A BIGGER HOUSE THAN EVERYBODY ELSE IN SOUTH PARK?

TOKEN'S FATHER: BECAUSE WE HAVE MORE MONEY, SON.

TOKEN: I KNOW, BUT WHY?

TOKEN'S FATHER: BECAUSE WE WENT TO GRADUATE SCHOOL AND THEREFORE HAVE MORE LUCRATIVE JOBS THAN MOST PEOPLE IN TOWN. FOR INSTANCE, YOUR MOTHER IS A CHEMIST FOR A PHARMACEUTICAL COMPANY, WHEREAS YOUR FRIEND ERIC CARTMAN'S MOTHER IS A CRACK WHORE. ONE PAYS MORE THAN THE OTHER.

PRIEST: ERIC, GOD COULD SURE USE THAT MONEY FOR A BIGGER CHURCH.
CARTMAN: I THINK GOD HAS PLENTY OF MONEY.

KYLE: WAIT, ISN'T THERE SOME RULE ABOUT NOT GETTING INTO CARS WITH STRANGERS?

CARTMAN: NO, NOT WHEN MONEY'S INVOLVED, STUPID.

CARTMAN: STAN, DON'T YOU KNOW THE FIRST LAW OF PHYSICS? ANYTHING THAT'S FUN COSTS AT LEAST $8.

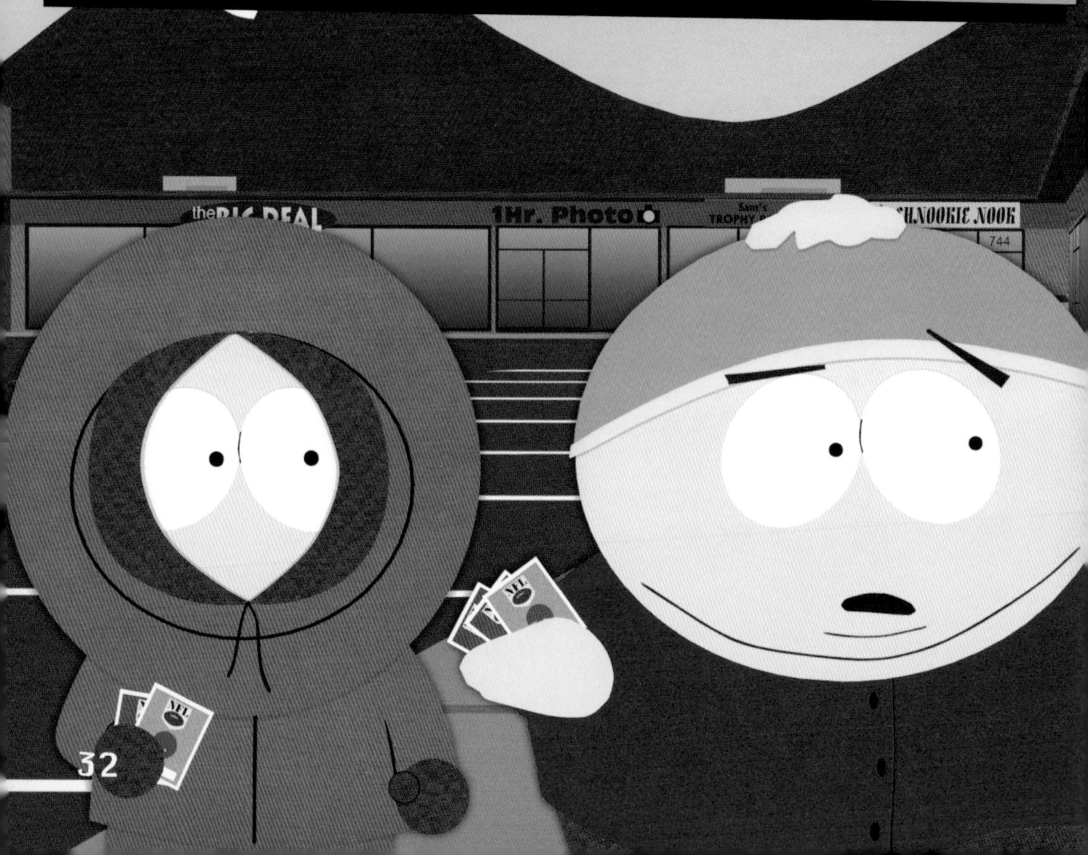

He DELIVERS!

CARTMAN: NO FREELOADERS ARE GONNA TAKE MY HARD-EARNED CASH.

KYLE: YOUR GRANDMA LEFT IT TO YOU. YOU DIDN'T EARN IT.

CARTMAN: DIDN'T EARN IT? WHAT ABOUT ALL THOSE YEARS I SPENT MAKING GRANDMA LIKE ME? ALL THE WET SPIT-FILLED KISSES I PUT UP WITH? THE CONSTANT SMELL OF ASPIRIN AND PEE? DON'T TELL ME I DIDN'T EARN IT YOU SON OF A BITCH!

CARTMAN: EVERYONE KNOWS THAT ONLY POOR PEOPLE GET LICE.
SNACKY S'MORES
T

BEST FRIENDS FOREVER

STAN: JUST BECAUSE WE RIP ON YOU FOR BEING RICH DOESN'T MEAN WE DON'T LIKE YOU.

KYLE: YEAH, WE'RE GUYS, DUDE. WE FIND SOMETHING ABOUT ALL OUR FRIENDS TO RIP ON.

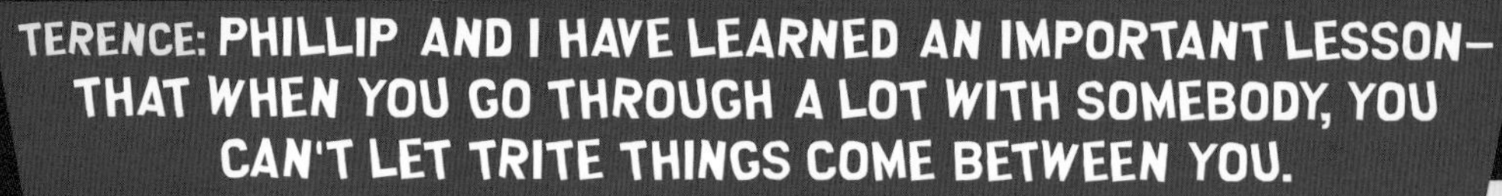

PHILLIP: THAT'S RIGHT TERENCE, YOU SHOULD ONLY LET THINGS COME BETWEEN YOUR ASS CHEEKS!

CARTMAN: CRAIG, DUDE, I RAN AWAY FROM HOME. YOU'RE THE FIRST PERSON I CAME TO. I KNEW YOU'D TAKE ME IN OFF THE STREETS.

CRAIG: BUT I HATE YOU.

CARTMAN: SHOULD THAT REALLY MATTER AT A TIME LIKE THIS?

STAN: DUDE, WE NEVER THOUGHT YOU WERE COOL.

CARTMAN: THAT'S NOT TRUE. YOU'RE JUST SAYING THAT.

KYLE: NO, REALLY. WE'VE ALWAYS THOUGHT YOU SUCK.

JIMMY: YEAH, NOTHING'S CHANGED. OUR OPINION OF YOU CAN'T POSSIBLY GO ANY LOWER.

CARTMAN: YOU'RE ALL JUST SAYING THAT TO MAKE ME FEEL BETTER.

GOTH KID: IF YOU WANNA BE ONE OF THE NON-CONFORMISTS, ALL YOU HAVE TO DO IS DRESS JUST LIKE US AND LISTEN TO THE SAME MUSIC WE DO.

CARTMAN: WE'RE IN THIS TOGETHER, CRAIG! IF BUTTERS TELLS ON US THEN WE'RE GONNA TELL ON YOU. THAT'S THE NINJA CODE!

STAN: DUDE, WE DON'T HAVE ANY MUSICAL TALENT.

CARTMAN: THAT DIDN'T STOP ANY OF THE OTHER BOY BANDS, DUMB ASS.

CULTURAL DIVERSITY KICKS ASS

JUDGE: I AM MAKING AN EXAMPLE OF YOU TO SEND A MESSAGE OUT TO PEOPLE EVERYWHERE: THAT IF YOU WANT TO HURT ANOTHER HUMAN BEING, YOU'D BETTER MAKE DAMN SURE THEY'RE THE SAME COLOR AS YOU ARE.

EAGLE VALLEY
LOVELAND
GYP
KYLE: TOKEN SINGS?
CARTMAN: OF COURSE HE SINGS; HE'S BLACK.

SGT. GUY: WHY IS IT THAT US POLICEMEN AROUND THE COUNTRY HAVE SUCH A PASSION FOR FRAMING WEALTHY AFRICAN AMERICANS WITH CRIMES THEY DIDN'T COMMIT?

DETECTIVE HARRIS: OH, I . . . I GUESS I'VE NEVER THOUGHT ABOUT WHY, SIR. **WE JUST DO IT.**

MISS STEVENS: ALL RIGHT, THAT DOES IT. ERIC CARTMAN, YOU RESPECT OTHER CULTURES.
CARTMAN: I WASN'T SAYING ANYTHING ABOUT THEIR CULTURE. I WAS JUST SAYING THEIR CITY SMELLS LIKE ASS.

MR. HAT: WITH GENETIC ENGINEERING WE CAN CORRECT ALL OF GOD'S HORRIBLE MISTAKES . . . LIKE GERMAN PEOPLE.

STAN: I'M STARTING TO THINK THAT MAYBE IT'S WRONG TO PUT SOMEONE WHO THINKS THEY'RE A VIETNAMESE PROSTITUTE ONTO A BULL.

CARTMAN: DO BRITISH PEOPLE COUNT AS AN ETHNICITY?

STAN: NAH.

STEPHEN ABOOTMAN: WHEN YOU THINK OF CANADA, WHAT'S THE ONE THING THAT COMES TO MIND?
CARTMAN: GAYNESS.

UNCLE JIMBO:

HELL, EVERYTHING'S LEGAL IN MEXICO.
IT'S THE AMERICAN WAY.

MR. GARRISON: **A HAIKU IS JUST LIKE A NORMAL AMERICAN POEM, EXCEPT IT DOESN'T RHYME AND IT'S TOTALLY STUPID.**

SMITTY: I DIDN'T KNOW THEY WAS INVITING REDNECKS TO THIS EVENT.
STAN: WE'RE NOT REDNECKS.
KYLE: YEAH! THAT'S TEXANS, BUTTHOLE!

HIPPIES SUCK

JANET RENO: LOOK, PEOPLE HAVE IT SO GOOD IN AMERICA THAT THEY GET BORED VERY EASILY. AND WHEN PEOPLE GET BORED, THEY START PROTESTING THINGS.

STAN: ENVIRONMENTAL ACTIVISTS DON'T USE LOGIC OR REASON.

NEWS REPORTER #1: WE'RE HERE LIVE IN SAN JOSE, COSTA RICA, WHERE HUNDREDS OF RICH AMERICANS HAVE GATHERED FOR THE SAVE THE RAINFOREST SUMMIT. EVERYONE IS HERE SO THEY CAN FEEL GOOD ABOUT THEMSELVES AND ACT LIKE THEY AREN'T THE ONES RESPONSIBLE FOR THE RAINFOREST'S PERIL.

NEWS REPORTER #2: THAT'S RIGHT, BOB!

KYLE: HYBRID CARS DON'T CAUSE SMUGNESS. PEOPLE DO.

STAN: WHAT DO WE WANT?
KYLE: GAYS IN SCOUTS!
SCOTCH
STAN: WHEN DO WE WANT IT?
TIMMY: TIMMY!

Mascot!

CARTMAN: VOTE FOR **TURD SANDWICH**. THIS IS THE MOST IMPORTANT ELECTION OF YOUR LIFE. TURD SANDWICH BRINGS THE HOPE FOR CHANGE. A VOTE FOR **TURD SANDWICH** IS A VOTE FOR TOMORROW.

Az By Cx Dw Ev Fu Gt Hs Ir Jq Kp Lo Mn Nm Ol Pk Qj Ri Sh Tg
CARTMAN: I'M NOT BRINGING IN FOOD FOR POOR PEOPLE, SCREW THEM.
WENDY: DON'T YOU WANT TO HELP THOSE WHO ARE LESS FORTUNATE?
CARTMAN: HEY GUYS, DO YOU HEAR SOMETHING? I THINK I HEAR THE FLOWER CHILDREN CALLING.
CANNED FOOD DRIVE

MAYOR: ALRIGHT PEOPLE, WE NEED TO COME UP WITH ANSWERS. THERE ARE **HOMELESS PEOPLE** SPROUTING UP ALL OVER TOWN. WHAT ARE WE SUPPOSED TO DO?

MR. VALMER: WELL, I SORT OF HAD AN IDEA. WE COULD GIVE THE HOMELESS ALL **DESIGNER SLEEPING BAGS** AND **MAKEOVERS.** AT LEAST THAT WAY THEY'D BE PLEASANT TO LOOK AT.

GOD
BLESS
AMERICA

HUNTIN' AND KILLIN'

KYLE: YOU REALLY THINK THAT YOUR CIVILIZATION IS BETTER THAN OURS? YOU PEOPLE PLAY GAMES BY KILLING ANIMALS AND OPPRESS WOMEN!
OTHER KID: IT'S BETTER THAN A CIVILIZATION THAT SPENDS ITS TIME WATCHING MILLIONAIRES WALKING DOWN THE RED CARPET AT THE EMMYS.
STAN: HE'S GOT US THERE, DUDE.

RANDY: THE STRENGTH OF THIS COUNTRY IS TO DO ONE THING AND SAY ANOTHER.

STAN: THIS IS AMERICA AND IN AMERICA, IF SOMETHING SUCKS, YOU'RE SUPPOSED TO BE ABLE TO GET YOUR MONEY BACK!

CARTMAN: REMEMBER BILL BEELICHECK. HEAD COACH OF THE NEW ENGLAND PATRIOTS. HE'S WON THREE SUPER BOWLS. HOW? HE CHEATED. HE EVEN GOT CAUGHT CHEATING AND NOBODY CARED! HE PROVED THAT IN AMERICA, IT'S ALRIGHT TO CHEAT, AS LONG AS YOU CHEAT YOUR WAY TO THE TOP.

CARTMAN: GOD BLESS THOSE MEN THAT FIGHT FOR THEIR FREEDOM. GOD BLESS THOSE MEN. AND GOD BLESS THE CONFEDERACY!

CARTMAN: I'D RATHER US BE CHINESE THAN A NATION OF UNETHICAL DICK SHOOTERS. THINK ABOUT IT.

MR. GARRISON: ERIC, STANLEY JUST MIGHT LEAD OUR TEAM TO VICTORY AGAINST THE MIDDLE PARK COWBOYS FOR THE FIRST TIME IN DECADES. AND WE TREAT STAR ATHLETES BETTER 'CAUSE THEY'RE BETTER PEOPLE.

KYLE: ONE-FOURTH OF AMERICANS ARE RETARDS.

STAN: YEAH, AT LEAST ONE-FOURTH.

KYLE LETS TAKE A TEST SAMPLE. THERE'S FOUR OF US, YOU'RE A RETARD, AND THAT'S ONE-FOURTH.

ARE YOU THERE, GOD? IT'S ME, JESUS.

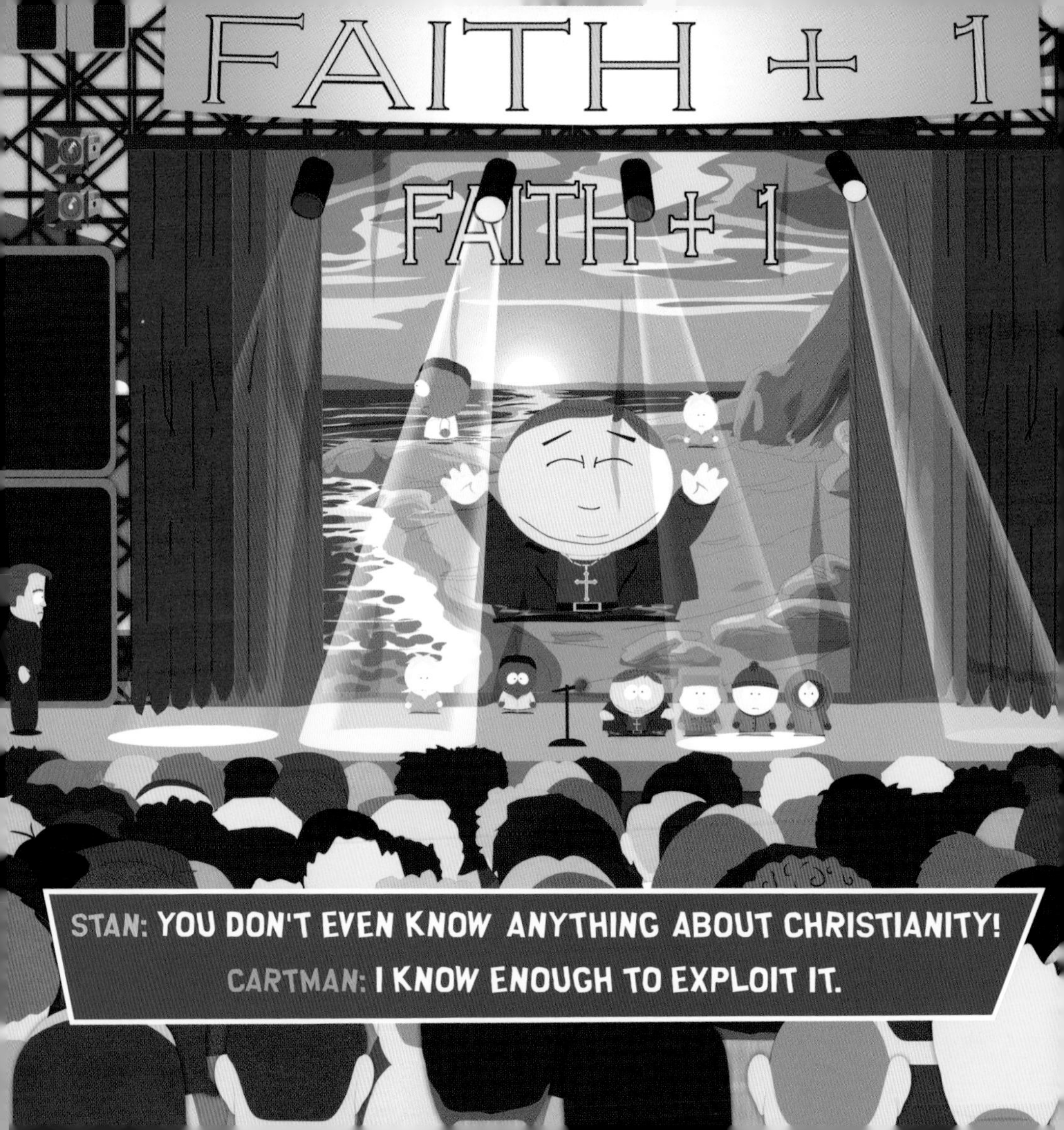
FAITH + 1
FAITH + 1
STAN: YOU DON'T EVEN KNOW ANYTHING ABOUT CHRISTIANITY!
CARTMAN: I KNOW ENOUGH TO EXPLOIT IT.

STAN: NO, NO, NO. I GET IT. JESUS WANTED US TO EAT HIM, BUT HE DIDN'T WANT US TO BE CANNIBALS, SO HE TURNED HIMSELF INTO CRACKERS AND THEN TOLD PEOPLE TO EAT HIM.

RANDY MARSH:

OH BOY, NOW THAT WE'RE ATHEISTS, WE DON'T HAVE TO PRAY FOR OUR FOOD!

BUTTERS:

IF I'M BI-CURIOUS AND I'M SOMEHOW MADE FROM GOD, THEN I FIGURE GOD MIGHT BE A LITTLE BI-CURIOUS HIMSELF!

POPE:
ALRIGHT, THAT DOES IT BILL. I'M PRETTY SURE KILLING JESUS IS NOT VERY CHRISTIAN.

FATHER MAXI:

THEY CRUCIFIED OUR LORD AND SAVIOR. IF YOU DON'T GO TO HELL FOR CRUCIFYING OUR SAVIOR THEN WHAT THE HELL DO YOU GO TO HELL FOR?

CARTMAN:

HEAVEN COULD BE LIKE THE PIXIE FAIRIES OF BUBBLE YUM™ FOREST. YOU ONLY SEE THEM IF YOU REALLY BELIEVE IN THEM.

TOM: SANTA CLAUS AND LEPRECHAUNS ARE IMAGINARY, BUT JESUS AND HELL ARE REAL.

SCIENTIST 1: WELL THEN, WHAT ABOUT BUDDHA?

TOM: WELL, OF COURSE HE'S IMAGINARY.

MR. GARRISON: **THE HARE KRISHNAS ARE TOTALLY GAY.**

KYLE: I FINALLY FIGURED IT OUT. YOU SEE, IF SOMEONE LIKE CARTMAN CAN GET A MILLION DOLLARS AND HIS OWN THEME PARK, THEN THERE IS NO GOD. THERE IS NO GOD, DUDE.

STAN: COULDN'T EVOLUTION BE THE ANSWER TO "HOW" AND NOT THE ANSWER TO "WHY?"

MRS. GARRISON: UH-OH, RETARD ALERT. RETARD ALERT, CLASS. DO YOU BELIEVE IN A FLYING SPAGHETTI MONSTER TOO, BUBBLEHEAD?

CARTMAN: DON'T BE SAD, BUTTERS. WHAT AWAITS EACH PERSON IN HEAVEN IS ETERNAL BLISS, DIVINE REST, AND TEN THOUSAND DOLLARS CASH.

CARTMAN: I'VE SOMETIMES LOOKED AT PEOPLE WITH DISABILITIES AS PEOPLE GOD PUT HERE ON EARTH FOR MY AMUSEMENT.

JIMMY: MY MOM SAYS GOD HAS A PLAN FOR EVERYONE. I GUESS I WAS PLAN B.

BRIAN: WELL I THINK SCIENTOLOGY CAN REALLY MAKE YOU HAPPY AGAIN.

STAN: WELL WHAT DO I DO?

BRIAN: IT'S VERY SIMPLE. WE JUST NEED $240.

CLASS
DISMISSED

CARTMAN: THIS JUST GOES TO SHOW THAT HARD WORK DOESN'T PAY OFF. I'M GOING TO BE A HOMELESS DRUG ADDICT FROM NOW ON!

MR. ADLER: YOU ARE HERE BECAUSE YOU ARE AMERICA'S FUTURE. YOU MAY SOMEDAY BE DOCTORS, OR LAWYERS, OR SCIENTISTS. MOST OF YOU, HOWEVER, WILL BE PUMPING GAS OR CUTTING SHEET METAL AND THAT'S WHY WE HAVE SHOP CLASS.

STAN: ART IS JUST KINDA FOR GAYWADS.
BUTTERS: I LOVE ART CLASS!
STAN: SEE.

MS. CHOKSONDIK: ALRIGHT, CHILDREN, LET'S SETTLE DOWN. AS I'M SURE YOU ALL REMEMBER, TODAY WE ARE GOING TO CONTINUE OUR BIOLOGY LESSON BY DISSECTING AN ORGANISM.

WENDY: UH, MS. CHOKSONDIK, AREN'T MANATEES ENDANGERED?

MS. CHOKSONDIK: THEY SURE ARE, WENDY, AND THAT IS WHY WE MUST LEARN WHAT'S INSIDE THEM.

CARTMAN: BUT YOU KNOW, WE'VE ALL LEARNED SOMETHING YOU GUYS. WE CAN NEVER PERSECUTE LIVING BEINGS AND FORCE THEM INTO HIDING. IT'S WRONG.

KYLE: AND YOU DON'T SEE ANY PARALLEL BETWEEN THAT AND ANYTHING ELSE IN HISTORY?

CARTMAN: MMMM NOPE, I HAVE NO IDEA WHAT YOU'RE TALKING ABOUT, KYLE.

DRUGS
ARE BAD
MMKAY?

SNACKY CAKES

SNACKY
CAKES

POLICE
SWAT
POLICE
CHICAGO POLICE
SWAT NEGOTIATOR
TOWELIE: I LEARNED I SHOULDN'T GET HIGH TO COME UP WITH IDEAS. I SHOULD COME UP WITH IDEAS AND THEN GET HIGH TO REWARD MYSELF.

CARTMAN: DRUGS ARE BAD BECAUSE IF YOU DO DRUGS YOU'RE A HIPPIE AND HIPPIES SUCK.

COUNSELOR: SO JUST TRY AND STAY POSITIVE, STAY AWAY FROM DRUGS AND ALCOHOL, AND IN THE MEANTIME, I'M GOING TO PUT YOU ON A HEAVY REGIMEN OF PROZAC.

CARTMAN: OH, NO THANKS, WE DON'T DO THAT STUFF.

KID 2: YOU WILL. THERE'S A REASON MOST SAN FRANCISCO KIDS TAKE A LOT OF DRUGS.

KID 3: IT'S THE ONLY THING THAT ALLOWS US TO DEAL WITH OUR PARENTS WALKING AROUND LOVING THE SMELL OF THEIR OWN FARTS ALL OF THE TIME.

CHEF: LOOK, CHILDREN,
THIS IS ALL I'M GOING TO SAY ABOUT DRUGS.
STAY AWAY FROM THEM.
THERE'S A TIME AND A PLACE FOR EVERYTHING—
AND IT'S CALLED COLLEGE.

KYLE: HEY STAN, NOW THAT TERRANCE AND PHILIP HAS BEEN TAKEN OFF THE AIR, WHAT ARE WE GOING TO DO FOR ENTERTAINMENT?

STAN: I DUNNO . . . WE COULD START BREATHING GAS FUMES . . .

CARTMAN: MY UNCLE SAYS THAT SMOKING CRACK IS KINDA COOL . . .

CARTMAN: THESE ARE WHAT WE CALL THE GIGGLING STONERS. PRETTY COMMON FORM OF HIPPIE USUALLY FOUND IN THE ATTICS. PROBLEM IS, IF YOU SEE ONE HIP-PIE, THERE'S PROBABLY A WHOLE LOT MORE YOU'RE NOT SEEING.

I'M CALLING CHILD PROTECTIVE SERVICES

I'm with stupid
SP
SP
SP
SP
SOUTH PARK
SOUTH PARK
SOUTH PARK
SOUTH PARK

KYLE:
WHEN PEOPLE HAVE CHILDREN, THEY HAVE TO GROW UP!

STAN: PARENTS CAN BE PRETTY CRUEL SOMETIMES, DUDE. THEY GET OFF ON IT.

BUTTERS: **MY DAD ALWAYS SAID, "IT'S OK TO LOSE. BUT IF YOU DON'T TRY, WELL THEN, YOU'RE GROUNDED, MISTER."**

STAN'S DAD: I'M GONNA BE THERE FOR YOU AND I'LL BE ROOTING LOUDER THAN ANYBODY SAYING, "THAT'S MY SON!" AND JUST REMEMBER, STAN. WIN OR LOSE . . . THOSE ARE YOUR TWO OPTIONS: WIN OR LOSE.

BUTTERS' DAD: THAT'S RIGHT. THERE'S NO REASON TO BE AFRAID OF THINGS THAT AREN'T **REAL**. THERE'S PLENTY OF **REAL** THINGS TO BE SCARED OF.

LIKE SUPER AIDS.

JIMMY'S DAD: JIMMY, WE'VE TOLD YOU BEFORE—GOD MADE YOU THE WAY HE DID FOR A REASON.

JIMMY: RIGHT, BECAUSE YOU AND MOM USED TO MAKE FUN OF CRIPPLED KIDS IN HIGH SCHOOL.

JIMMY'S DAD: THAT'S RIGHT. YOU WERE SENT HERE THROUGH THE VENGEFUL AND ANGRY HAND OF GOD TO TEACH YOUR MOTHER AND I A LESSON. AND THAT'S A BIG RESPONSIBILITY, SON.

STAN'S DAD: I KNOW YOU THINK THIS SET OF BOOBS IS IMPORTANT NOW, BUT THOSE BOOBS WILL BE REPLACED BY ANOTHER SET OF BOOBS. BOOBS WILL COME AND GO. AND THEN SOMEDAY, YOU'LL MEET A PAIR OF BOOBS THAT YOU WANT TO MARRY. AND THOSE BECOME THE BOOBS THAT MATTER MOST.

STAN'S MOM: I LOVE YOU.

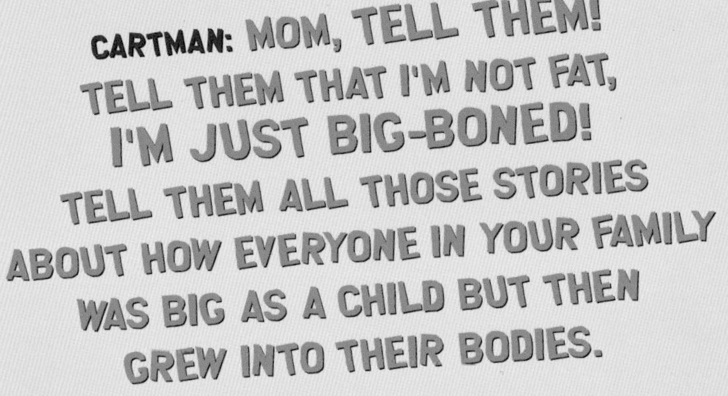

CARTMAN'S MOM: OH, SWEETIE . . .
THOSE WERE ALL LIES.
YOU'RE JUST FAT.

WHO PUT HIS HOO HOO DILLY IN YOUR CHA CHA?

SOUTH PARK
SOUTH PARK

PIP: JOE, DO YOU KNOW ANYTHING ABOUT GIRLS?
JOE: SURE. THEY'RE THOSE THINGS WITH VAGINAS IN THEM.

MR. MACKEY: "QUEEF" IS A VAGINAL EXPULSION OF GAS, MKAY.

Dw Ev Fu Gt Hs Ir Jq Kp Lo Mn Nm Ol Pk Qj Ri Sh Tg Uf

FACTS OF LIFE

BLAIR

JO

MR. GARRISON:

YEAH, I TELL YOU BOYS . . . WOMEN CAN KILL. POONTANG'S EXPENSIVE. THAT'S WHY WHEN IT COMES TO CHICKS, I JUST SCREW THEM AND LEAVE 'EM. I SAY, "GET OUT MY BEDROOM, POONTANG, BEFORE YOU SUCK MY LIFE DRY!"

KYLE: YOU NEED TO HAVE A LIFE. HAVE FUN. THEN RUIN IT BY HAVING A SERIOUS RELATIONSHIP.

CARTMAN: IT'S A MAN'S OBLIGATION TO STICK HIS BONERATION IN A WOMAN'S SEPARATION. THIS SORT OF PENETRATION WILL INCREASE THE POPULATION OF THE YOUNGER GENERATION.

MS. CHOKSONDIK: ALL RIGHT, GIRLS. YESTERDAY WE WENT OVER THE MYRIAD OF DISEASES YOU CAN GET FROM BOYS, BUT TODAY WE'RE GOING TO TALK ABOUT THE MOST HORRIBLE DISEASE THEY CAN GIVE YOU OF ALL: **PREGNANCY!**

TOKEN:

FIVE MIDGETS SPANKING A MAN COVERED IN THOUSAND ISLAND DRESSING. IS THAT MAKING LOVE?

CARTMAN: DON'T BE JEALOUS, GUYS! THIS DOESN'T MEAN WE CAN'T STILL HANG OUT. IT JUST MEANS I'VE MATURED FASTER THAN YOU. YOU'LL GET YOUR PUBES GUYS, SOMEDAY.

KYLE: CARTMAN, YOU DON'T BUY PUBES, YOU GROW THEM YOURSELF!

DOCTOR:

MAKING BREASTS LARGER IS A BEAUTIFUL AND WONDERFUL THING. MAKING THEM SMALLER IS INSANE.

GOD: YOU WILL HIT PUBERTY WHEN THE TIME IS RIGHT, BUT YOU WILL NEVER HAVE A PERIOD BECAUSE YOU ARE A MAN WITH TITTIES.

BEBE'S MOM:
PART OF BEING A WOMAN IS HAVING A FRIEND ONE DAY AND CALLING HER A SLUT THE NEXT.

CARTMAN:

OKAY, OUR MISSION FAILED BUT WE LEARNED A LOT. PRIMARILY THAT GIRLS DO NOT HAVE BALLS.

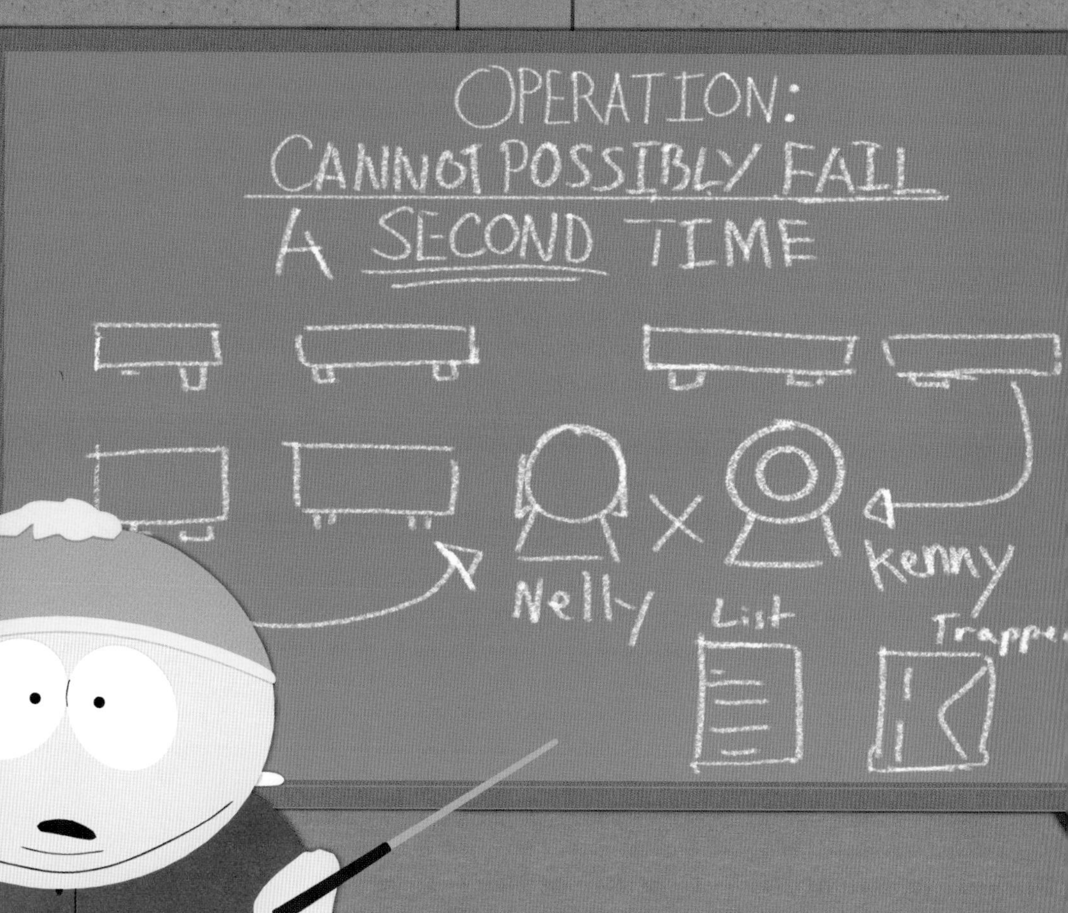
OPERATION:
CANNOT POSSIBLY FAIL
A SECOND TIME
Nelly
Kenny
List
Trapper

ACKNOWLEDGMENTS

COMPILED BY:

SUSAN HURWITZ ARNESON

ERICK THORPE

ADDITIONAL CONTRIBUTIONS BY:

MARK MUNLEY

JACK ZEGARSKI

SPECIAL THANKS:

ANNE GAREFINO

TROY BYNUM

STACEY GEE

DEBRA KRASSNER

ROB LAQUINTA

MARGARET MILNES

RAINA MOORE

STEVE RAIZES

We got what you need
COMEDY CENTRAL
OH MY GOD, THEY KILLED KENNY!
YOU BASTARDS!
HOW'D YOU LIKE ME TO KICK YOU IN THE NUTS?
THE COMPLETE ELEVENTH SEASON
UNCENSORED
BUTTERS
TIMMY
CARTMAN
...come and get us.
www.comedycentral.com/shop & other kick ass retailers